Imagine POETRY Anthology

SERIES EDITORS
Margaret Iveson
Samuel Robinson

EDITORIAL CONSULTANT
Alan Simpson

LITERATURE CONSULTANT
Rivka Cranley

TEACHER CONSULTANTS
Bill Talbot
Karen Brust
Janet Hancock
Wendy Mathieu
Kathy Smith

PRENTICE HALL CANADA INC.

ISBN 0-13-017971-X
© 1993 by Prentice-Hall Canada Inc., Scarborough, Ontario

Anthologists: Sean Armstrong, Monica Kulling, Mary Beth Leatherdale
Researchers: Monika Croydon, Catherine Rondina

A Ligature Book
Cover Illustration: *Music Conductor by Seashore* © Jerry Lofaro/ The Image Bank

Canadian Cataloguing in Publication Data
Main entry under title:

Imagine poetry : anthology

(MultiSource)
ISBN 0-13-017971-X

1. Children's poetry. 2. Poetics – Juvenile
literature. I. Iveson, Margaret L., 1948–
II. Robinson, Sam, 1937– . III. Series.
PZ8.3.I553 1993   j808.81   C92–095224–0

Printed and bound in Canada
    8 9 10   FP   02 01 00

Poetry

What is Poetry? Who knows?
Not a rose, but the scent of the rose;
Not the sky, but the light in the sky;
Not the fly, but the gleam of the fly;
Not the sea, but the sound of the sea;
Not myself, but what makes me
See, hear, and feel something that prose
Cannot: and what it is, who knows?

ELEANOR FARJEON

Contents

Poetry

I had no centimes
and rushed into the shop.
closest to the quay.
"I want some paper," I all but shouted
to the middle-aged shopkeeper
arranging her morning display
of vegetables and fruits;
she looked at me as if to say,
"What's that to me, I've done
without lots of things I've wanted."
nevertheless she quietly asked me
what I needed the paper for

"I'm writing a poem," I told her,
not feeling grand at all
but self-conscious and absurd
among the fruit and vegetable smells

"That's serious," was all she said,
and disappearing
behind the counter
bobbed up, the needed sheets in her hand

IRVING LAYTON

"Progress"

Earth poet
So busy
weaving
    magic
into words

so busy
placing
    patterns
quilting
    stars
so busy
making
    the sun
dance
so busy
singing
    your songs
in circles
so busy
tipping
    moons
in dreams

Earth poet
so busy
touching
    the land
scape
mad modern man
must take me
look at
cold steel spires
stealing earth and sun
    dance.

EMMA LaROCQUE

Autobiographia Literaria

When I was a child
I played by myself in a
corner of the schoolyard
all alone.

I hated dolls and I
hated games, animals were
not friendly and birds
flew away.

If anyone was looking
for me I hid behind a
tree and cried out "I am
an orphan."

And here I am, the
center of all beauty!
writing these poems!
Imagine!

FRANK O'HARA

Mirror

When you look	kool uoy nehW
into a mirror	rorrim a otni
it is not	ton si ti
yourself you see,	,ees uoy flesruoy
but a kind	dnik a tub
of apish error	rorre hsipa fo
posed in fearful	lufraef ni desop
symmetry.	.yrtemmys

JOHN UPDIKE

How Everything Happens

(Based on a Study of the Wave)

                                                happen.
                                        to
                                    up
                            stacking
                                is
                        something
When nothing is happening
When it happens
                        something
                                    pulls
                                        back
                                            not
                                                to
                                                    happen.
When   has happened.
        pulling back   stacking up
                    happens
            has happened   stacks up
When it   something   nothing
                        pulls back while
Then nothing is happening.
                                            happens.
                                    and
                            forward
                        pushes
                            up
                    stacks
            something
Then

MAY SWENSON

The Moth's Serenade

Voice 1	*Voice 2*
Porch	Porch
light,	light,
hear my plight!	hear my plight!
I drink your light	
like nectar	like nectar
	Dream of you
by day	by day
Gaze in your eyes	
all night	all night
Porch light!	Porch light!
	Bright paradise!
I am	I am
your seeking	
circling	seeking
sighing	circling
lovesick	sighing
knight	
You are	You are
	my soul's
my soul's	desire
desire	my prize
my prize	my eyes'
	delight
Porch Light!	Porch light!
My shining star!	

"Keep back," they say
I can't!
"Don't touch," they say

Porch light!
Let's clasp
Let's kiss
Let's marry for a trice!

Porch light!
Let's meet
Let's merge
Let's live for love!
For light!

My compass needle's North!
"Keep back," they say

"Don't touch," they say
I must!
Porch light!
Let's kiss
Let's clasp
Let's marry for a trice!

Porch light!
Let's merge
Let's meet

For light!

PAUL FLEISCHMAN

Warning: (A Found Poem)

This contract limits our liability.
Read it.
We accept no responsibility
For loss of or damage to you
Or your contents.
We do not take custody of you,
But only rent space.
No in or out privileges,
Valid for life purchased only,
Detach stub.

YVONNE BOETTCHER

A Wish

I want to climb the santol tree*
That grows beside my bedroom window
And get a santol fruit.
I want to climb the tree at night
And get the moon the branches hide.
Then I shall go to bed, my pockets full,
One with the fruit, the other with the moon.

TOMAS SANTOS

---

*The santol tree has sharp-tasting red fruit used in preserves.

Winter

Animals are restless
Birds are in flight,
Butterflies are not out.
Leaves; a gray blanket,
Winter lurks near.

Icy fingers grasp the world.
Snow falls; graceful, beautiful,
            undisturbed.
Silence creeps about.

JOHN CONSTANT

THE
WINNER

by Peg Kehret, from a collection
of monologues for young actors

There was a competition at our school last year. A poetry competition. Anyone who wanted to could write a poem and enter it in the contest. The best ten were printed in a booklet and the first-prize winner received twenty-five dollars and a framed certificate.

I wanted to win that contest more than I ever wanted anything in my life. Not for the twenty-five dollars, although I could have used the money. I wanted to win because deep down inside me I wanted to be a writer and I wasn't sure if I had any talent. I thought if I won first prize in a poetry competition, it would mean I do have some ability.

I'm not real good at most other things. Especially sports. Everyone else jogs and works out. They lift weights and play tennis or volleyball. I hate exercising. I'm always the last one to be chosen when we pick teams for baseball or basketball. And the only reason I passed

Physical Education last year was because my gym partner lied for me and said I'd done the required three push-ups when I could barely manage one.

Maybe that's why the poetry contest was so important to me. When you're really rotten at most things, you want to be extra-good at the few things you care about.

I worked on my contest entry every day for two weeks. I wrote seven different poems and threw all of them away. I wrote about butterflies and kittens and the way I feel when I hear certain kinds of music. None of my poems was any good. I crumpled them up and threw them in my wastebasket. I wanted them to be beautiful, and instead, they were awkward and crude.

But I didn't give up. I kept writing. I revised and changed the words around and thought up new ideas for poems.

And then, on the last night before the contest deadline, I wrote a poem that I knew was good. It was a simple poem, but every time I read it, I got goosebumps on my arms. I knew it was the best writing I'd ever done. I called it "Unicorn Magic" and I entered it in the contest the next morning.

The winner was not announced until two weeks later. During those two weeks, I floated in a special dream, imagining how it would be to sit at the awards program in the school auditorium and hear my name announced as the first-prize winner in the poetry competition.

On the day of the awards, I couldn't eat breakfast. I wore my new grey pants, the ones that make me look thinner than I am. I got up half an hour early so I'd have time to wash my hair.

Before the winner was announced, the principal read the names of the authors of the ten best poems. Mine was one of them. My heart began to pound and my mouth got all dry. Then he announced the winner: first prize to Kathy Enderson for her poem titled "Goldfish Jubilee."

When Kathy's name was called, she shrieked and jumped up and all her friends screamed and cheered. I just sat there, stunned. I couldn't believe "Unicorn Magic" had lost when it made me get goosebumps every time I read it. Maybe I wasn't going to be a writer, after all. Maybe I had no talent. If Kathy Enderson, who laughs at dirty jokes and flirts with all the guys and thinks being a cheerleader is the most important thing in the world, if Kathy can write better poetry than I can, then I might as well give it up forever.

Except I couldn't. I went home that day and wrote a poem about how much it hurt to lose the competition. When I read the poem again the next morning, I got goosebumps on my arms and I knew I would keep on writing, even if I never won any awards.

I studied Kathy's poem in the booklet. I had to admit it was good.

That summer, long after the poetry competition was over and school was out, I was looking through some magazines in the public library and I came across a poem titled "Goldfish Jubilee." For one awful moment, I thought Kathy had not only won the contest, she'd actually had her poem published. Then I saw the author's name. Andrew Billings. "Goldfish Jubilee" by Andrew Billings. The poem was the same; the author was not.

I looked at the date on the magazine. It was published a month before our poetry competition.

Should I show it to the principal and demand that the poems be judged again? Should I call Kathy Enderson and tell her I knew she'd cheated? What good would it do? That special moment in the school auditorium, when the winner's name was announced, was over. It was too late.

I hate Kathy Enderson for what she did, but I feel sorry for her, too. She has a certificate that says *First Prize, Poetry Competition,* and she has the twenty-five dollars, but she doesn't know how it feels to read her very own poem and get goosebumps on her arms.

And she'll never know.

Name Giveaway

That teacher gave me a new name . . . again.
She never even had a feast, or, giveaway!

Still I do not know what "George" means,
   and now she calls me: "Phillip."

TWO SWANS ASCENDING FROM STILL WATERS
   must be
too hard for her to remember—

PHILLIP WILLIAM GEORGE

STANLEY
KUNITZ
talks about poetry

by Stanley Kunitz, from *Poetspeak*,
an anthology

When I was a boy in Worcester, Massachusetts, I used to travel miles on my bike in order to go swimming in a lake outside the city limits that was known as Webster Lake. The reason I went there, in preference to more accessible bodies of water, was that I had discovered, while browsing through a local history at the public library, that the Indians long ago had given that lake a name, reputed to be the longest lake name in the world. I practiced how to say it and to this day still have it on my tongue. This is how it goes: Lake Chauggogagogmanchauggagogchabunagungamaugg . . . meaning I-fish-on-my-side   you-fish-on-your-side   nobody-fishes-in-the-middle. That knowledge gave me a secret power. I suppose it is in the nature of the poet, beginning in childhood, to love the sounds of language. Others may swim in Webster Lake, but poets swim in Lake Chauggogagogmanchauggagogchabunagungamaugg. . . .

A poem is at once the most primitive and the most sophisticated use of language. It has its roots in magic—in the spell over things delivered by the priest or shaman of the tribe. The words of a poem go back to the beginnings of the human adventure when the first syllables were not spoken but sung or chanted or danced. So it is that poetry always seems about to burst into song, to break into dance, but the secret of the poet's mastery is that he refrains from crossing over—the words stay words, they remain language.

Above all, poetry is intended for the ear. It must be felt to be understood, and before it can be felt it must be heard. Poets listen for their poems, and we, as readers, must listen in turn. If we listen hard enough, who knows? —we too may break into dance, perhaps for grief, perhaps for joy.

"Never try to explain," I say in the course of one of my poems, and that seems to me excellent advice to follow. When I read interpretations of my own work I am often puzzled by what others have found in it. A poem does not tell what it means, even to its maker. A prime source of its power is that it has its roots in the secrecy of a life and that it means more than it says. And a poem demands of its readers that they must come out to meet it, at least as far as it comes out to meet them, so that *their* meaning may be added to its. A common fallacy is to think that a poem begins with a meaning which then gets dressed up in words. On the contrary, a poem is language surprised in the act of changing into meaning. . . .

The occasion of "End of Summer" is still vivid to me. I was living in the country, in Bucks County, Pennsylvania, and one day, at the turning of the season, while I was hoeing in the field, I heard a clamor in the sky and looked

upward to see wave after wave of wild geese thundering
south in their V-formations. In the actual process of writing, the geese flew out of the poem, but even now, when
I read the lines aloud, I can hear the beating of their
wings. . . .

End of Summer

An agitation of the air,
A perturbation of the light
Admonished me the unloved year
Would turn on its hinge that night.

I stood in the disenchanted field
Amid the stubble and the stones,
Amazed, while a small worm lisped to me
The song of my marrow-bones.

Blue poured into summer blue,
A hawk broke from his cloudless tower,
The roof of the silo blazed, and I knew
That part of my life was over.

Already the iron door of the north
Clangs open: birds, leaves, snows
Order their populations forth,
And a cruel wind blows.

STANLEY KUNITZ

Seventeen Syllables

by Hisaye Yamamoto, from *Counterpoint,*
a magazine of Asian studies

The first Rosie knew that her mother had taken to writing poems was one evening when she finished one and read it aloud for her daughter's approval. It was about cats, and Rosie pretended to understand it thoroughly and appreciate it no end, partly because she hesitated to disillusion her mother about the quantity and quality of Japanese she had learned in all the years now that she had been going to Japanese school every Saturday (and Wednesday, too, in the Summer). Even so, her mother must have been skeptical about the depth of Rosie's understanding, because she explained afterwards about the kind of poem she was trying to write.

See, Rosie, she said, it was a *haiku,* a poem in which she must pack all her meaning into seventeen syllables only, which were divided into three lines of five, seven, and five syllables. In the one she had just read, she had tried to capture the charm of a kitten, as well as comment on the superstition that owning a cat of three colors meant good luck.

"Yes, yes, I understand. How utterly lovely," Rosie said, and her mother, either satisfied or seeing through the deception and resigned, went back to composing.

The truth was that Rosie was lazy; English lay ready on the tongue but Japanese had to be searched for and examined, and even then put forth tentatively (probably to meet with laughter). It was so much easier to say yes, yes, even when one meant no, no. Besides, this was what was in her mind to say: I was looking through one of your magazines from Japan last night, Mother, and towards the back I found some *haiku* in English that delighted me. There was one that made me giggle off and on until I fell asleep—

> It is morning, and lo!
> I lie awake, comme il faut,
> sighing for some dough.

Now, how to reach her mother, how to communicate the melancholy song? Rosie knew formal Japanese by fits and starts, her mother had even less English, no French. It was much more possible to say yes, yes. . . .

The Future of Poetry in Canada

Some people say we live in a modern mechanized nation
where the only places that matter
are Toronto, Montreal, and maybe Vancouver;
but I myself prefer Goodridge, Alberta,
a town where electricity arrived in 1953,
the telephone in 1963.

In Goodridge, Alberta,
the most important social events
have been the golden wedding anniversaries of the residents.
There have been a Garden Club, a Junior Grain Club, and a
    Credit Union,
and there have been farewell parties,
well attended in spite of the blizzards.

Weather is important in Goodridge.
People remember the time they threshed in the snow,
and the winter the temperature fell to seventy below.

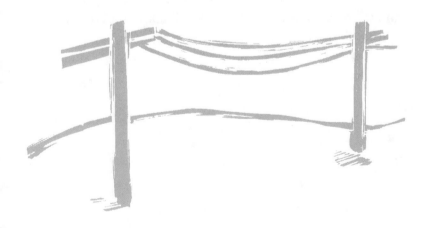

They also remember the time
the teacher from White Rat School
piled eight children in his car
and drove them, as a treat,
all the way to Edmonton;
where they admired the Jubilee Auditorium
and the Parliament Buildings
and visited the CNR wash rooms
but were especially thrilled
going up and down in an elevator.

I hope at least one poet
in the next generation
comes from Goodridge, Alberta.

ELIZABETH BREWSTER

Great Things Have Happened

We were talking about the great things
that have happened in our lifetimes;
and I said, "Oh, I suppose the moon landing
was the greatest thing that has happened
in my time." But, of course, we were all lying.
The truth is the moon landing didn't mean
one-tenth as much to me as one night in 1963
when we lived in a three-room flat in what once
    had been
the mansion of some Victorian merchant prince
(our kitchen had been a clothes closet, I'm sure),
on a street where by now nobody lived
who could afford to live anywhere else.
That night, the three of us, Claudine, Johnnie and me,
woke up at half-past four in the morning
and ate cinnamon toast together.

"Is that all?" I hear somebody ask.

Oh, but we were silly with sleepiness
and, under our windows, the street-cleaners
were working their machines and conversing in
    Italian, and
everything was strange without being threatening,
even the tea-kettle whistled differently
than in the daytime: it was like the feeling
you get sometimes in a country you've never visited
before, when the bread doesn't taste quite the same,

the butter is a small adventure, and they put
paprika on the table instead of pepper,
except that there was nobody in this country
except the three of us, half-tipsy with the wonder
of being alive, and wholly enveloped in love.

ALDEN NOWLAN

Now Elizabeth

Now Elizabeth knew as well as you
that everything has its place.
But she could care less
and her room was a mess,
so her mom said this to her face:

"Now Elizabeth, PLEASE, I'm down on my knees,
can't you neaten it up a bit!"
Elizabeth said, "Of course,"
but the place was worse
and her mom left the room in a fit.

"If you can't clean your room with a vacuum or broom
it's much too dirty, you know."
DO NOT ENTER on the door
was what the sign bore,
and Liz said, "Is that so!"

She had great fun and when she was done
she had a little bit more.
But after three days (about)
Liz began to pout
and the fun turned into a bore.

The bed was prickly, the floor was stickly
and there was no room to sit.
And up in a corner
(not little Jack Horner)
was a web that a spider did knit.

Liz tidied and fussed and wiped away dust
and then she did that some more.
She washed, shook and rushed
and neatened and brushed
and then tore the sign from the door.

And when everything was as neat as a pin
Liz hung up a very big sign:
                                        COME IN

P.S.
Dedicated to my mom.

JEANNE HOLMES

The Snow Tramp

When it snowed
in Winnipeg
my mother would look
out the kitchen window
and say
I wish I was a gypsy.

She would put on
her moccasins and
sweaters, wrap a scarf
around her neck, shoulder
her snowshoes and go
tramping
in Kildonan park.

That evening when
my father came home
he found us all supperless,
he was angry and worried
but he opened a can of soup
and fed us.

When my mother
came home it was late
and dark; she shook
the snow from her hair
and wondered how it happened
we didn't know she had gone
tramping
in Kildonan park.

My father scolded,
but my mother's soul
was far away
wrapped like a gift
in stars and snow,
and all night long
her gypsy tunes sang
and danced in the wind
around our house.

MIRIAM WADDINGTON

The Wreck of the Edmund Fitzgerald

The legend lives on from the Chippewa on down of the big lake
    they called Gitche Gumee.
The lake, it is said, never gives up her dead, when the skies of
    November turn gloomy.
With a load of iron ore 26,000 tons more than the Edmund
    Fitzgerald weighed empty
That good ship and true was a bone to be chewed when the
    gales of November came early.

The ship was the pride of the American side, coming back from
    some mill in Wisconsin.
As the big freighters go it was bigger than most, with a crew
    and good captain well seasoned,
Concluding some terms with a couple of steel firms, when they
    left fully loaded for Cleveland.
And later that night when the ship's bell rang, could it be the
    north wind they'd bin feelin'?

The wind in the wires made a tattletale sound and a wave
    broke over the railing,
And ev'ry man knew as the captain did too, 'twas the witch of
    November come stealin'.
The dawn came late and the breakfast had to wait, when the
    gales of November came slashin'.
When afternoon came it was freezin' rain, in the face of a
    hurricane west wind.

When suppertime came the old cook came on deck sayin',
    "Fellas it's too rough t'feed ya."
At seven p.m. a main hatchway caved in;
    he said, "Fellas, it's been good t'know ya."

The captain wired in he had water comin' in and the good ship
    and crew was in peril,
And later that night when 'is lights went outta sight came the
    wreck of the Edmund Fitzgerald.

Does anyone know where the love of God goes when the waves
    turn the minutes to hours?
The searchers all say they'd have made Whitefish Bay if they'd
    put fifteen more miles behind 'er.
They might have split up or they might have capsized; they might
    have broke deep and took water.
And all that remains is the faces and the names of the wives
    and the sons and the daughters.

Lake Huron rolls, Superior sings, in the rooms of her ice-water
    mansion,
Old Michigan steams like a young man's dreams, the islands
    and bays are for sportsmen.
And farther below, Lake Ontario takes in what Lake Erie can
    send her,
And the iron boats go as the mariners all know, with the gales
    of November remembered.

In a musty old hall in Detroit they prayed in the Maritime
    Sailors' Cathedral,
The church bell chimed 'til it rang 29 times for each man on
    the Edmund Fitzgerald.
The legend lives on from the Chippewa on down of the big lake
    they called Gitche Gumee.
Superior, they said, never gives up her dead when the gales of
    November come early!

GORDON LIGHTFOOT

Richard Cory

Whenever Richard Cory went down town,
    We people on the pavement looked at him:
He was a gentleman from sole to crown,
    Clean favored, and imperially slim.

And he was always quietly arrayed,
    And he was always human when he talked;
But still he fluttered pulses when he said,
    "Good-morning," and he glittered when he walked.

And he was rich—yes, richer than a king,
    And admirably schooled in every grace:
In fine, we thought that he was everything
    To make us wish that we were in his place.

So on we worked, and waited for the light,
    And went without the meat, and cursed the bread;
And Richard Cory, one calm summer night,
    Went home and put a bullet through his head.

EDWIN ARLINGTON ROBINSON

Richard Cory

They say that Richard Cory owns one-half of this whole town
with political connections to spread his wealth around
born into society, a banker's only child.
He had everything a man could want: power, grace and style.

Chorus:
But I work in his factory and I curse the life I'm living,
And I curse my poverty. And I wish that I could be,
Oh I wish that I could be
Oh I wish that I could be,
Richard Cory.

The papers print his picture almost everywhere he goes.
Richard Cory at the opera. Richard Cory at a show.
And the rumours of his parties. And the orgies on his yacht.
Oh he surely must be happy with everything he's got.

Chorus

He freely gave to charity. He hath the common touch.
And they were grateful for his patronage, and they thanked him
very much.
So my mind was filled with wonder when the evening headlines
read:
Richard Cory went home last night and put a bullet through his
head.

Chorus

PAUL SIMON

"Out, Out—" *

The buzz-saw snarled and rattled in the yard
And made dust and dropped stove-length sticks
    of wood,
Sweet-scented stuff when the breeze drew across it.
And from there those that lifted eyes could count
Five mountain ranges one behind the other
Under the sunset far into Vermont.
And the saw snarled and rattled, snarled and rattled,
As it ran light, or had to bear a load.
And nothing happened: day was all but done.
Call it a day, I wish they might have said
To please the boy by giving him the half hour
That a boy counts so much when saved from work.
His sister stood beside them in her apron
To tell them "Supper." At the word, the saw,
As if to prove saws knew what supper meant,
Leaped out at the boy's hand, or seemed to leap—
He must have given the hand. However it was,
Neither refused the meeting. But the hand!
The boy's first outcry was a rueful laugh,
As he swung toward them holding up the hand
Half in appeal, but half as if to keep
The life from spilling. Then the boy saw all—

---

*Frost's title is a quotation from the famous passage in Shakespeare's play
Macbeth, (act 5, scene 5, lines 23–28) in which Macbeth reacts to the sudden
death of his wife. The passage is below.

> . . . Out, out, brief candle!
> Life's but a walking shadow, a poor player
> That struts and frets his hour upon the stage
> And then is heard no more. It is a tale
> Told by an idiot, full of sound and fury,
> Signifying nothing. . . .

Since he was old enough to know, big boy
Doing a man's work, though a child at heart—
He saw all spoiled. "Don't let them cut my hand
    off—
The doctor, when he comes. Don't let him, sister!"
So. But the hand was gone already.
The doctor put him in the dark of ether.
He lay and puffed his lips out with his breath.
And then—the watcher at his pulse took fright.
No one believed. They listened at his heart.
Little—less—nothing!—and that ended it.
No more to build on there. And they, since they
Were not the one dead, turned to their affairs.

ROBERT FROST

I Go Along

by Richard Peck, from *Connections*,
a book of short stories for young adults

Anyway, Mrs. Tibbetts comes into the room for second
period, so we all see she's still in school. This is the spring
she's pregnant, and there are some people making some
bets about when she's due. The smart money says she'll
make it to Easter, and after that we'll have a sub teaching
us. Not that we're too particular about who's up there at
the front of the room, not in this class.

Being juniors, we also figure we know all there is to
know about sex. We know things about sex no adult ever
heard of. Still, the sight of a pregnant English teacher
slows us down some. But she's married to Roy Tibbetts, a
plumber who was in the service and went to jump school,
so that's okay. We see him around town in his truck.

And right away Darla Craig's hand is up. It's up a lot.
She doesn't know any more English than the rest of us,
but she likes to talk.

"Hey, Mrs. Tibbetts, how come they get to go and we don't?"

She's talking about the first-period people, the Advanced English class. Mrs. Tibbetts looks like Darla's caught her off base. We never hear what a teacher tells us, but we know this. At least Darla does.

"I hadn't thought," Mrs. Tibbetts says, rubbing her hand down the small of her back, which may have something to do with being pregnant. So now we're listening, even here in the back row. "For the benefit of those of you who haven't heard," she says, "I'm taking some members of the—other English class over to the college tonight, for a program."

The college in this case is Bascomb College at Bascomb, a thirty-mile trip over an undivided highway.

"We're going to hear a poet read from his works."

Somebody halfway back in the room says, "Is he living?" And we all get a big bang out of this.

But Mrs. Tibbetts just smiles. "Oh, yes," she says, "he's very much alive." She reaches for her attendance book, but this sudden thought strikes her. "Would anyone in this class like to go too?" She looks up at us, and you see she's being fair, and nice.

Since it's only the second period of the day, we're all feeling pretty good. Also it's a Tuesday, a terrible TV night. Everybody in the class puts up their hands. I mean everybody. Even Marty Crawshaw, who's already married. And Pink Hohenfield, who's in class today for the first time this month. I put up mine. I go along.

Mrs. Tibbetts looks amazed. She's never seen this many hands up in our class. She's never seen anybody's hand except Darla's. Her eyes get wide. Mrs. Tibbetts has really great eyes, and she doesn't put anything on them. Which is something Darla could learn from.

But then she sees we have to be putting her on. So she just says, "Anyone who would like to go, be in the parking lot at five-thirty. And eat first. No eating on the bus."

Mrs. Tibbetts can drive the school bus. Whenever she's taking the advanced class anywhere, she can go to the principal for the keys. She can use the bus anytime she wants to, unless the coach needs it.

Then she opens her attendance book, and we tune out. And at five-thirty that night I'm in the parking lot. I have no idea why. Needless to say, I'm the only one here from second period. Marty Crawshaw and Pink Hohenfield will be out on the access highway about now, at 7-Eleven, sitting on their hoods. Darla couldn't make it either. Right offhand I can't think of anybody who wants to ride a school bus thirty miles to see a poet. Including me.

The advanced-English juniors are milling around behind school. I'm still in my car, and it's almost dark, so nobody sees me.

Then Mrs. Tibbetts wheels the school bus in. She's got the amber fogs flashing, and you see the black letters along the yellow side: CONSOLIDATED SCHOOL DIST. She swings in and hits the brakes, and the doors fly open. The advanced class starts to climb aboard. They're more orderly than us, but they've got their groups too. And a couple of smokers. I'm settling behind my dashboard. The last kid climbs in the bus.

And I seem to be sprinting across the asphalt. I'm on the bus, and the door's hissing shut behind me. When I swing past the driver's seat, I don't look at Mrs. Tibbetts, and she doesn't say anything. I wonder where I'm supposed to sit.

They're still milling around in the aisle, but there are plenty of seats. I find an empty double and settle by the window, pulling my ball cap down in front. It doesn't take us long to get out of town, not this town. When we go past 7-Eleven, I'm way down in the seat with my hand shielding my face on the window side. Right about then, somebody sits down next to me. I flinch.

"Okay?" she says, and I look up, and it's Sharon Willis.

I've got my knee jammed up on the back of the seat ahead of me. I'm bent double, and my hand's over half my face. I'm cool, and it's Sharon Willis.

"Whatever," I say.

"How are you doing, Gene?"

I'm trying to be invisible, and she's calling me by name.

"How do you know me?" I ask her.

She shifts around. "I'm a junior, you're a junior. There are about fifty-three people in our whole year. How could I not?"

Easy, I think, but don't say it. She's got a notebook on her lap. Everybody seems to, except me.

"Do you have to take notes?" I say, because I feel like I'm getting into something here.

"Not really," Sharon says, "but we have to write about it in class tomorrow. Our impressions."

I'm glad I'm not in her class, because I'm not going to have any impressions. Here I am riding the school bus for the gifted on a Tuesday night with the major goddess girl in school, who knows my name. I'm going to be clean out of impressions because my circuits are starting to fail.

Sharon and I don't turn this into anything. When the bus gets out on the route and Mrs. Tibbetts puts the pedal to the metal, we settle back. Sharon's more or less in with a group of the top girls around school. They're not even cheerleaders. They're a notch above that. The rest of them are up and down the aisle, but she stays put. Michelle Burkholder sticks her face down by Sharon's ear and says, "We've got a seat for you back here. Are you coming?"

But Sharon just says, "I'll stay here with Gene." Like it happens every day.

I look out the window a lot. There's still some patchy snow out in the fields, glowing gray. When we get close to the campus of Bascomb College, I think about staying on the bus.

"Do you want to sit together," Sharon says, "at the program?"

I clear my throat. "You go ahead and sit with your people."

"I sit with them all day long," she says.

At Bascomb College we're up on bleachers in a curtained-off part of the gym. Mrs. Tibbetts says we can sit any-where we want to, so we get very groupy. I look up, and here I am sitting in these bleachers, like we've gone to State in the play-offs. And I'm just naturally here with Sharon Willis.

We're surrounded mainly by college students. The dean of Bascomb College gets up to tell us about the grant they got to fund their poetry program. Sharon has her notebook flipped open. I figure it's going to be like a class, so I'm tuning out when the poet comes on.

First of all, he's only in his twenties. Not even a beard, and he's not dressed like a poet. In fact, he's dressed like me: Levi's and Levi's jacket. Big heavy-duty belt buckle. Boots, even. A tall guy, about a hundred and eighty pounds. It's weird, like there could be poets around and you wouldn't realize they were there.

But he's got something. Every girl leans forward. College girls, even. Michelle Burkholder bobs up to zap him with her flash camera. He's got a few loose-leaf pages in front of him. But he just begins.

"I've written a poem for my wife," he says, "about her."

Then he tells us this poem. I'm waiting for the rhyme, but it's more like talking, about how he wakes up and the sun's bright on the bed and his wife's still asleep. He watches her.

> "Alone," he says, "I watch you sleep
> Before the morning steals you from me,
> Before you stir and disappear
> Into the day and leave me here
> To turn and kiss the warm space
> You leave beside me."

He looks up and people clap. I thought what he said was a little too personal, but I could follow it. Next to me Sharon's made a note. I look down at her page and see it's just an exclamation point.

He tells us a lot of poems, one after another. I mean, he's got poems on everything. He even has one about his truck:

> "Old buck-toothed, slow-to-start mama,"

something like that. People laugh, which I guess is okay. He just keeps at it, and he really jerks us around with his poems. I mean, you don't know what the next one's going to be about. At one point they bring him a glass of water, and he takes a break. But mainly he keeps going.

He ends up with one called "High School."

"On my worst nights," he says, "I dream myself back.
I'm the hostage in the row by the radiator, boxed in,
Zit-blasted, and they're popping quizzes at me.
I'm locked in there, looking for words
To talk myself out of being this young
While every girl in the galaxy
Is looking over my head, spotting for a senior.
On my really worst nights it's last period
On a Friday and somebody's fixed the bell
So it won't ring:
    And I've been cut from the team,
    And I've forgotten my locker combination,
    And I'm waiting for something damn it to hell
    To happen."

And the crowd goes wild, especially the college people. The poet just gives us a wave and walks over to sit down on the bottom bleacher. People swarm down to get him to sign their programs. Except Sharon and I stay where we are.

"That last one wasn't a poem," I tell her. "The others were, but not that one."

She turns to me and smiles. I've never been this close to her before, so I've never seen the color of her eyes.

"Then write a better one," she says.

We sit together again on the ride home.

"No, I'm serious," I say. "You can't write poems about zits and your locker combination."

"Maybe nobody told the poet that," Sharon says.

"So what are you going to write about him tomorrow?" I'm really curious about this.

"I don't know," she says. "I've never heard a poet reading before, not in person. Mrs. Tibbetts shows us tapes of poets reading."

"She doesn't show them to our class."

"What would you do if she did?" Sharon asks.

"Laugh a lot."

The bus settles down on the return trip. I picture all these people going home to do algebra homework, or whatever. When Sharon speaks again, I almost don't hear her.

"You ought to be in this class," she says.

I pull my ball cap down to my nose and lace my fingers behind my head and kick back in the seat. Which should be answer enough.

"You're as bright as anybody on this bus. Brighter than some."

We're rolling on through the night, and I can't believe I'm hearing this. Since it's dark, I take a chance and glance at her. Just the outline of her nose and her chin, maybe a little stubborn.

"How do you know I am?"

"How do you know you're not?" she says. "How will you ever know?"

But then we're quiet because what else is there to say? And anyway, the evening's over. Mrs. Tibbetts is braking for the turnoff, and we're about to get back to normal. And I get this quick flash of tomorrow, in second period with Marty and Pink and Darla, and frankly it doesn't look that good.

Mississippi Winter IV

My father and mother both
used to warn me
that 'a whistling woman and a crowing
hen would surely come to
no good end.' And perhaps I should
have listened to them.
But even at the time I knew
that though my end probably might
not
be good
I must whistle
like a woman undaunted
until I reached it.

ALICE WALKER

Silent, but . . .

I may be silent, but
I'm thinking.
I may not talk, but
Don't mistake me for a wall.

TSUBOI SHIGEJI

Geraldine Moore

THE POET

by Toni Cade Bambara

Geraldine paused at the corner to pull up her knee socks. The rubber bands she was using to hold them up made her legs itch. She dropped her books on the sidewalk while she gave a good scratch. But when she pulled the socks up again, two fingers poked right through the top of her left one.

"That stupid dog," she muttered to herself, grabbing her books and crossing against traffic. "First he chews up my gym suit and gets me into trouble, and now my socks."

Geraldine shifted her books to the other hand and kept muttering angrily to herself about Mrs. Watson's dog, which she minded two days a week for a dollar. She passed the hot-dog man on the corner and waved. He shrugged as if to say business was very bad.

Must be, she thought to herself. *Three guys before you had to pack up and forget it. Nobody's got hot-dog money around here.*

Geraldine turned down her street, wondering what her sister Anita would have for her lunch. She was glad she didn't have to eat the free lunches in high school any more. She was sick of the funny-looking tomato soup and the dried-out cheese sandwiches and those oranges that were more green than orange.

When Geraldine's mother first took sick and went away, Geraldine had been on her own except when Miss Gladys next door came in on Thursdays and cleaned the apartment and made a meat loaf so Geraldine could have dinner. But in those days Geraldine never quite managed to get breakfast for herself. So she'd sit through social studies class, scraping her feet to cover up the noise of her stomach growling.

Now Anita, Geraldine's older sister, was living at home waiting for her husband to get out of the Army. She usually had something good for lunch—chicken and dumplings if she managed to get up in time, or baked ham from the night before and sweet-potato bread. But even if there was only a hot dog and some baked beans— sometimes just a TV dinner if those soap operas kept Anita glued to the TV set—anything was better than the noisy school lunchroom where monitors kept pushing you into a straight line or rushing you to the tables. Anything was better than that.

Geraldine was almost home when she stopped dead. Right outside her building was a pile of furniture and some boxes. That wasn't anything new. She had seen people get put out in the street before, but this time the ironing board looked familiar. And she recognized the big, ugly sofa standing on its arm, its underbelly showing the hole where Mrs. Watson's dog had gotten to it.

Miss Gladys was sitting on the stoop, and she looked

up and took off her glasses. "Well, Gerry," she said slowly, wiping her glasses on the hem of her dress, "looks like you'll be staying with me for a while." She looked at the men carrying out a big box with an old doll sticking up over the edge. "Anita's upstairs. Go on up and get your lunch."

Geraldine stepped past the old woman and almost bumped into the superintendent. He took off his cap to wipe away the sweat.

"Darn shame," he said to no one in particular. "Poor people sure got a hard row to hoe."

"That's the truth," said Miss Gladys, standing up with her hands on her hips to watch the men set things on the sidewalk.

Upstairs, Geraldine went into the apartment and found Anita in the kitchen.

"I dunno, Gerry," Anita said. "I just don't know what we're going to do. But everything's going to be all right soon as Ma gets well." Anita's voice cracked as she set a bowl of soup before Geraldine.

"What's this?" Geraldine said.

"It's tomato soup, Gerry."

Geraldine was about to say something. But when she looked up at her big sister, she saw how Anita's face was getting all twisted as she began to cry.

That afternoon, Mr. Stern, the geometry teacher, started drawing cubes and cylinders on the board. Geraldine sat at her desk adding up a column of figures in her notebook—the rent, the light and gas bills, a new gym suit, some socks. Maybe they would move somewhere else, and she could have her own room. Geraldine turned the squares and triangles into little houses in the country.

"For your homework," Mr. Stern was saying with his

back to the class, "set up your problems this way." He wrote GIVEN: in large letters, and then gave the formula for the first problem. Then he wrote TO FIND: and listed three items they were to include in their answers.

Geraldine started to raise her hand to ask what all these squares and angles had to do with solving real problems, like the ones she had. *Better not,* she warned herself, and sat on her hands. *Your big mouth got you in trouble last term.*

In hygiene class, Mrs. Potter kept saying that the body was a wonderful machine. Every time Geraldine looked up from her notebook, she would hear the same thing. "Right now your body is manufacturing all the proteins and tissues and energy you will need to get through tomorrow."

And Geraldine kept wondering, *How? How does my body know what it will need, when I don't even know what I'll need to get through tomorrow?*

As she headed down the hall to her next class, Geraldine remembered that she hadn't done the homework for English. Mrs. Scott had said to write a poem, and Geraldine had meant to do it at lunchtime. After all, there was nothing to it—a flower here, a raindrop there, moon, June, rose, nose. But the men carrying off the furniture had made her forget.

"And now put away your books," Mrs. Scott was saying as Geraldine tried to scribble a poem quickly. "Today we can give King Arthur's knights a rest. Let's talk about poetry."

Mrs. Scott moved up and down the aisles, talking about her favorite poems and reciting a line now and then. She got very excited whenever she passed a desk and could pick up the homework from a student who had remembered to do the assignment.

"A poem is your own special way of saying what you feel and what you see," Mrs. Scott went on, her lips moist. It was her favorite subject.

"Some poets write about the light that . . . that . . . makes the world sunny," she said, passing Geraldine's desk. "Sometimes an idea takes the form of a picture—an image."

For almost half an hour, Mrs. Scott stood at the front of the room, reading poems and talking about the lives of the great poets. Geraldine drew more houses, and designs for curtains.

"So for those who haven't done their homework, try it now," Mrs. Scott said. "Try expressing what it is like to be . . . to be alive in this . . . this glorious world."

"Oh, brother," Geraldine muttered to herself as Mrs. Scott moved up and down the aisles again, waving her hands and leaning over the students' shoulders and saying, "That's nice," or "Keep trying." Finally she came to Geraldine's desk and stopped, looking down at her.

"I can't write a poem," Geraldine said flatly, before she even realized she was going to speak at all. She said it very loudly, and the whole class looked up.

"And why not?" Mrs. Scott asked, looking hurt.

"I can't write a poem, Mrs. Scott, because nothing lovely's been happening in my life. I haven't seen a flower since Mother's Day, and the sun don't even shine on my side of the street. No robins come sing on my window sill."

Geraldine swallowed hard. She thought about saying that her father doesn't even come to visit any more, but changed her mind. "Just the rain comes," she went on, "and the bills come, and the men to move out our furniture. I'm sorry, but I can't write no pretty poem."

Teddy Johnson leaned over and was about to giggle

and crack the whole class up, but Mrs. Scott looked so serious that he changed his mind.

"You have just said the most . . . the most poetic thing, Geraldine Moore," said Mrs. Scott. Her hands flew up to touch the silk scarf around her neck. "'Nothing lovely's been happening in my life.'" She repeated it so quietly that everyone had to lean forward to hear.

"Class," Mrs. Scott said very sadly, clearing her throat, "you have just heard the best poem you will ever hear." She went to the board and stood there for a long time staring at the chalk in her hand.

"I'd like you to copy it down," she said. She wrote it just as Geraldine had said it, bad grammar and all.

Nothing lovely's been happening in my life.
I haven't seen a flower since Mother's Day,
And the sun don't even shine on my side of the street.
No robins come sing on my window sill.
Just the rain comes, and the bills come,
And the men to move out our furniture.
I'm sorry, but I can't write no pretty poem.

Mrs. Scott stopped writing, but she kept her back to the class for a long time—long after Geraldine had closed her notebook.

And even when the bell rang, and everyone came over to smile at Geraldine or to tap her on the shoulder or to kid her about being the school poet, Geraldine waited for Mrs. Scott to put the chalk down and turn around. Finally Geraldine stacked up her books and started to leave. Then she thought she heard a whimper—the way Mrs. Watson's dog whimpered sometimes—and she saw Mrs. Scott's shoulders shake a little.

What ugly is

i put on a man mask
and went among the people of earth
in search of what
ugly
means

many years the word had troubled
me, as i listened
over and over
to some of the approximately
four billion
mouth sounds
which these
animals
make

beauty i had come to understand
in stars
in eyes
the silver lapping of the oceans there
but ugly
what did it mean?

unrecognized
never speaking
but always listening
i walked their streets
and cities
i went into their starvations
their working places
deep in mines
i climbed a mountain
and looked into the writings
and holy codes
of their artists

but it wasn't until
i shared quarters with an actual family
and watched in shock
the upbringing of their young
that i realized
ugly
is what happens to something
you don't love
enough

ROBERT PRIEST

Buffalo in Compound: Alberta

The marsh flat where they graze
beside the stream is
late afternoon, serene
with slanted light: green leaves are
yellow: even
the mud shines

Placid, they bend down
silently to the grass;
when they move, the small birds
follow, settle almost
under their feet.

Fenced out but anxious
anyway, and glad our car is
near, we press
close to the wire
squares, our hands raised
for shields
against the sun, which is
everywhere

It was hard to see them
but we thought we saw
in the field near them, the god
of this place: brutal,
zeus-faced, his horned
head man-bearded, his
fused red eye turned inward
to cloudburst and pounded earth, the water-
falling of hooves fisted inside
a calm we would call madness.

Then they were going
in profile, one by one, their
firelit outlines fixed as carvings

backs to us now
they enter
the shade of the gold-edged trees

MARGARET ATWOOD

MARGARET ATWOOD

by Holly Hughes, from *Literary Cavalcade*,
a monthly magazine

Margaret Atwood once told an interviewer that when she began as a writer, she didn't take much interest in political matters, "but then I began to do what all novelists and some poets do; I began to describe the world around me." This, she claims, inevitably made her more aware of, and more vocal about, politics—at least about who wields power in our society and what uses he or she makes of that power. But perhaps this tendency was in her all along. In another interview she described her teenage writing as "lugubrious poems and grit-filled stories. I was big on grit. I had an eye for lawn litter and dog turds on sidewalks." From the very beginning, she observed the world intently, and carried on an instinctive quarrel with the way things are.

Born in Ottawa, in 1939, Margaret Atwood spent the first several years of her life constantly on the move around Canada, often in the wilderness, for her father was an entomologist, a scientist who studies insects. As an adult, she regrets that our society often robs girls of the self-confidence they need to succeed in a career, but her own upbringing luckily avoided that trap. Her mother was a grown-up tomboy, her brother hid snakes and worms in his bed, and both parents told her it was more important to use her mind than to catch a boyfriend. Although her schooling was frequently interrupted, she was always a great reader, and some of her childhood favorites were strong stuff—Edgar Allan Poe, *Gulliver's Travels,* Grimm's fairy tales, and piles of boys' adventure stories found in her grandfather's attic. She and her brother also collected loads of comic books, which their parents let them read only because they also read so many "real" books.

While she was still in high school, Margaret decided she was a writer and began to pound out poems and stories on an old typewriter. After college at the University of Toronto, then graduate school at Harvard University, she taught literature at various Canadian universities while launching her writing career, both as a poet and as a novelist (she has also published short stories, literary criticism, and some children's books). Her best-known work is the futuristic novel *A Handmaid's Tale,* which isn't really science fiction, but more like George Orwell's *1984* or Aldous Huxley's *Brave New World:* political fables set in a future world that deliver a warning about our present society.

As a woman, as a writer, as a Canadian, Atwood has often found herself cast in the role of an outsider, a role she fills with sharp wit and sly humor. For example, when critics disparage women writers for "writing like housewives" just because they are good at describing domestic details, Atwood retorts that a male writer could write the very same words and be praised for his "realism." But she also rails against feminist critics who demand that women writers always make female characters strong "role models," protesting that human beings—of either sex—are not perfect.

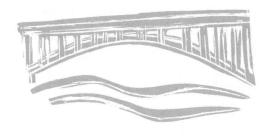

Lake of Bays

"Well, I'm not chicken . . ."
that skinny ten-year-old girl
balanced on the crazy-high railing
of the Dorset bridge:
                    suddenly
let go down
fifty feet into the water.

"That one will never grow up
to be a lady," my mother said
as we walked away;

but I'll remember
her brown body dropping like a stone
long after I've forgotten
many many ladies . . .

RAYMOND SOUSTER

This Is Just to Say

I have eaten
the plums
that were in
the icebox

and which
you were probably
saving
for breakfast

Forgive me
they were delicious
so sweet
and so cold

WILLIAM CARLOS WILLIAMS

Variations on a Theme by William Carlos Williams

1

I chopped down the house that you had been saving
    to live in next summer.
I am sorry, but it was morning, and I had nothing to do
and its wooden beams were so inviting.

2

We laughed at the hollyhocks together
and then sprayed them with lye.
Forgive me. I simply do not know what I am doing.

3

I gave away the money that you had been saving to
    live on for the next ten years.
The man who asked for it was shabby
and the firm March wind on the porch was so juicy and
    cold.

4

Last evening we went dancing and I broke your leg.
Forgive me. I was clumsy, and
I wanted you here in the wards, where I am a doctor.

KENNETH KOCH

in Just—

in Just—
spring   when the world is mud-
luscious the little
lame balloonman

whistles   far   and wee

and eddieandbill come
running from marbles and
piracies and it's
spring

when the world is puddle-wonderful

the queer
old balloonman whistles
far   and   wee
and bettyandisbel come dancing

from hop-scotch and jump-rope and

it's
spring
and
  the

        goat-footed
balloonMan   whistles
far
and
wee

e .   e .   c u m m i n g s

inappre ciation of eecumm ings

In just
winter   when the world is snowy
softand cloudy
BIG   SNOWFLAKES
fallingfalling   and falling
    land on the ground
children playing inthe snow
    having fun it's
       winter
when the season is cold
    the oldwind   whistles
fallingfalling   and falling
JoeandJane go   skiiiiiiiiiiiiiiiiiiing
    from hilltohill they skiiiiiii
it's
winter
  and
    the
snowflakes
      are
         fallingfalling
            andfalling
      down
to the ground.

LEONOR MENDES AND LINDA SHIMIZU

Eclipse

I looked the sun straight in the eye.
He put on dark glasses.

F. R. SCOTT

On Being Much Better Than Most and Yet Not Quite Good Enough

There was a great swimmer named Jack
Who swam ten miles out—and nine back.

JOHN CIARDI

For Anne

With Annie gone
Whose eyes to compare
With the morning sun?

Not that I did compare,
But I do compare
Now that she's gone.

LEONARD COHEN

Grandmother

The bright needles clicked;
The old woman's hands,
Quick, dextrous and expert,
Were a blur of colour.
"Your new gloves are finished."
She eased them on to
My short plump fingers.
"Now you can play in the snow."
I ran into the street, excited.
The gloves, soft, warm and dry
Were a magical source
Of safety and love.
Time drew on;
My winters grew colder;
The snow fell thicker.
Today my gloves
Are faded and thread-bare;
Her needles lie silent
And my hands are so cold.

ROBERT McGREGOR

Brief Encounter

our lines
intersected once
on a busy city street
You brushed by
and I wondered who you were
where you'd come from.
As I noticed
a mysterious intensity
in your face,
I wanted to know more about,
our eyes touched
for a moment

but we just kept on going
silently
on our
separate paths.

BETTINA GRASSMAN

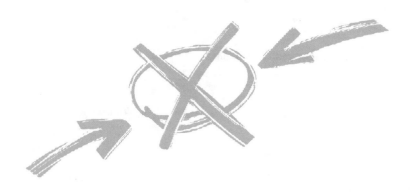

The City Is So Big

The city is so big
Its bridges quake with fear
I know, I have seen at night

The lights sliding from house to house
And trains pass with windows shining
Like a smile full of teeth

I have seen machines eating houses
And stairways walk all by themselves
And elevator doors opening and closing
And people disappear.

RICHARD GARCIA

City

In the morning the city
Spreads its wings
Making a song
In stone that sings.

In the evening the city
Goes to bed
Hanging lights
About its head.

LANGSTON HUGHES

Song Form

Morning uptown, quiet on the street,
no matter the distinctions that can be
made, quiet, very quiet, on the street.
Sun's not even up, just some kid and me,
skating, both of us, at the early sun, and
amazed there is grace for us, without our
having to smile too tough, or be very pleasant
even to each other. Merely to be mere, ly to be.

AMIRI BARAKA

Sing a Song of Subways

Sing a song of subways.
Never see the sun:
Four-and-twenty people
In room for one.

When the doors are opened—
Everybody run.

EVE MERRIAM

Pendulum

This lean commuter busies

Himself with being steady;

No matter where he is, he's

Been often there already.

JOHN UPDIKE

A Prairie Museum

city-dwellers
walk past leafless rose
and snowberry bushes
looking for crocuses
in the dead grass

as they walk
into its smallness
sky and horizon grow
buildings almost disappear

meadowlark sings
the sun's new song

crows exchange
their black song
with the white song
of seagulls

closer to the centre
single flowers
give way to bunches

pollen covered bees
crawl into blue heads

JIM TALLOSI

The Flame

One
red
cardinal

first
shooting
flame
of
spring

RAYMOND SOUSTER

The Tiger

The tiger
Has swallowed
A black sun,

In his cold
Cage he
Carries it still:

Black flames
Flicker through
His fur.

Black rays roar
From the centers
Of his eyes.

VALERIE WORTH

Autumn Cove

At Autumn Cove, so many white monkeys,
bounding, leaping up like snowflakes in flight!
They coax and pull their young ones down from
   the branches
to drink and frolic with the water-borne moon.

LI PO

Elephants

aren't any more important
than insects,

but I'm on the side
of elephants,

unless one of them tries
to crawl up my leg.

JOHN NEWLOVE

Lion

The lion is called the king
Of beasts. Nowadays there are
Almost as many lions
In cages as out of them.
If offered a crown, refuse.

KENNETH REXROTH

Riverdale Lion

Bound lion, almost blind from meeting their gaze and popcorn
the Saturday kids love you. It is their parents
who would paint your mane with polkadots to match their
    California shirts
and would trim your nails for tieclips.

Your few roars delight them. But they wish you would quicken
    your pace
and not disappear so often into your artificial cave
for there they think you partake of secret joys and race
through the jungle-green lair of memory
under an African sun as gold as your mane.

But you fool them. You merely suffer the heat and scatter the
    flies
with your tail. You never saw Africa.
The sign does not tell them that you were born here, in
    captivity,
that you are as much a Canadian as they are.

JOHN ROBERT COLOMBO

A mosquito in the cabin

Although you bash her,
    swat her, smash her,
and go to bed victorious,
    happy and glorious
    she will come winging,
    zooming and zinging,
    wickedly singing
over your bed.
You slap the air
    but she's in your hair
    cackling with laughter.
You smack your head,
    but she isn't dead—
    she's on the rafter.
She's out for blood—
    yours, my friend,
and she will get it, in the end.
She brings it first to boiling point,
    then lets it steam
With a fee, fi, fo and contented fum
    she sips it
    while you dream.

MYRA STILBORN

Sporting Words

this is supposed to be an exercise
although how words can be an exercise
I'll never know
I know basketball, baseball, volleyball
and best of all
zipping my old twelve-speed through traffic
but I'm not doing any of those things
I'm sitting by the window with the sun
waiting to begin
writing as an exercise

but it isn't easy
how can you run with a sentence?
how can you race down a paragraph
and fly round the turn
for the next page?
how can you push for all you're worth
to the final period?
I can't imagine words feeling that free
like wind on a light day and me bounding
with an energy that won't quit

I can't imagine words feeling that good
giving light and sky and
leaping lawns to speed across
making me feel like I've just
sunk the ball in the last seconds
a clean shot
I want sun in the words
and the wind's rush at my back while I write
but most of all the flying, I want the flying
the strong running with words

MONICA KULLING

The Skaters

Black swallows swooping or gliding
In a flurry of entangled loops and curves,
The skaters skim over the frozen river.
And the grinding click of their skates as they impinge
  upon the surface,
Is like the brushing together of thin wing-tips of silver.

JOHN GOULD FLETCHER

The Sidewalk Racer
OR
On the Skateboard

Skimming
an asphalt sea
I swerve, I curve, I
sway; I speed to whirring
sound an inch above the
ground; I'm the sailor
and the sail, I'm the
driver and the wheel
I'm the one and only
single engine
human auto
mobile.

LILLIAN MORRISON

Sound of Water

The sound of water is:
Rain,
Lap,
Fold,
Slap,
Gurgle,
Splash,
Churn,
Crash,
Murmur,
Pour,
Ripple,
Roar,
Plunge,
Drip,
Spout,
Slip,
Sprinkle,
Flow,
Ice,
Snow.

MARY O'NEILL

Peach

Touch it to your cheek and it's soft
as a velvet newborn mouse
who has to strive
to be alive.

Bite in. Runny
honey
blooms on your tongue—
as if you've bitten open
a whole hive.

ROSE RAUTER

My Fingers

My fingers are antennae.
Whatever they touch:
Bud, rose, apple
Cellophane, crutch—
They race the feel
Into my brain,
Plant it there and
Begin again.
This is how I knew
Hot from cold
Before I was even
Two years old.
This is how I can tell,
Though years away,
That elephant hide
Feels leathery grey.
My brain never loses
A touch I bring:
Frail of an eggshell,
Pull of a string,
Beat of a pulse
That tells me life
Thumps in a person
But not in a knife.
Signs that say:
"Please do not touch,"
Disappoint me
Very much.

MARY O'NEILL

Senses

Taste,
the dry, musky leaves,
which tamper with the air.
Lingering smoke,
the taste of ash.

Hear,
the clip of the shears,
as they prune the hedge.
Listen to the leaves,
as they throw a tantrum,
in the wind.

Smell,
the sweet fragrance,
from the soft, brown apples,
feasted by wasps.
The dusty corn
thrown from the yellow combine harvester.

See,
the rust colour,
painted through the garden.
See the bee
flying,
weighed down, with boots of yellow pollen.

Touch,
the leaves,
crumbling with dryness.
Feel the bitter night,
in the air,
of my autumn garden.

RUTH KINGSHOTT

Author Index

First Line Index for Poems

About the Authors

Margaret Atwood is a poet, novelist, and critic born in Ottawa in 1939. Her writing has won scores of awards.

Toni Cade Bambara is a short story writer and novelist, born in 1939 in New York City. Her themes revolve around African-American life and folklore.

Amiri Baraka has written plays, fiction, and essays, as well as poetry. Born in 1934, he is an influential part of the African-American literary culture.

Yvonne Boettcher graduated from Claremont Secondary School in Victoria, British Columbia, in 1991. She plans to attend university and continue writing.

Elizabeth Brewster was born in Chipman, New Brunswick, in 1922. Although her first volume of poetry was published in 1951, she has only recently become recognized for her poetry and stories about rural Canadian life.

John Ciardi (1916–1985) was a poet and magazine editor who wrote many essays, published two dictionaries, and wrote several books for children.

Leonard Cohen gained popularity as a singer and writer of love songs and protest songs in the 1960s and 70s. He was born in Montréal in 1934.

John Robert Colombo was born in 1936 in Kitchener, Ontario. He has written books of poetry and has also written plays and documentaries for the Canadian Broadcasting Company.

John Constant was a ten-year-old Canadian when his poem "Winter" was published in *Miracles: Poems by children of the English-speaking world* in 1966.

e. e. cummings (1894–1962) was born Edward Estlin Cummings in Boston. In addition to poetry, he wrote novels and children's stories, and painted.

Eleanor Farjeon lived in England from 1881 to 1965. She wrote hundreds of stories and poems, beginning at age seven.

Paul Fleischman grew up listening to his father read children's stories he had written. Now Fleischman writes his own award-winning books for young adults.

John Gould Fletcher (1886–1950) moved from his native England to rural Arkansas, where he wrote poetry about the power of simple country values to solve the problems of modern mechanized society.

Robert Frost (1874–1963) is best known for his poetry about New England life. He won four Pulitzer prizes for his many popular books.

Richard Garcia was born in 1941 in California. He writes poetry, children's stories, and books about Mexican-American culture.

Phillip William George is a member of the Nez Percé Nation in the state of Washington. As a young man he learned many of his ancestors' traditions, becoming an accomplished dancer. His writing has been widely published.

Bettina Grassman wrote this poem as a grade eleven student in Saskatoon. She has won local awards for her poetry.

Jeanne Holmes was a student when this poem was published in *Another Wordsandwich*, a collection of poetry by Canadian young people.

Holly Hughes, born in 1953, began her writing career in high school. Much of her writing and editing has been for student guidebooks and magazines.

Langston Hughes (1902–1967) was born in Joplin, Missouri. He became a leading figure in New York in the 1930s when African-American writers were beginning to receive recognition. Many of his verses have been set to music.

Peg Kehret began her writing career scripting radio commercials. Later, she wrote short stories, non-fiction, and poetry, much of it for young adults.

Ruth Kingshott has written for a book called *Young Worlds* by W. H. Smith, published in the United Kingdom.

Kenneth Koch (pronounced "coke,"), born in 1925, has shared his love of poetry with young and old audiences by teaching classes in elementary schools and nursing homes. A New Yorker, he has written many books.

Monica Kulling was born in Vancouver, British Columbia, and is an author for young readers. She has published two picture books and many poems.

Stanley Kunitz is a Pulitzer Prize–winning poet whose work has been known for sixty years. He was born in 1905 in Massachusetts.

Emma LaRocque contributed this poem to *Canadian Literature* magazine in 1990.

Irving Layton and his family moved from Romania to Montreal in 1913 when he was a year old. He is best known for his poetry of social protest.

Gordon Lightfoot is a composer, singer, and author born in 1938 in Orillia, Ontario. He has written over 400 songs and is one of Canada's top folksingers.

Robert McGregor was a fifteen-year-old student in Suffolk, England, when this poem was published in *Cadbury's Sixth Book of Children's Poetry* in 1988.

Leonor Mendes was born in 1978 and attends Moscrop Secondary School in Burnaby, British Columbia, where she enjoys reading and art.

Eve Merriam (1916–1992) worked as a poet, biographer, scriptwriter, editor, and teacher. Her award-winning poetry is often written for young audiences.

Lillian Morrison has spent many years working with young adults, in addition to publishing her own poetry.

John Newlove was born in Regina, Saskatchewan, in 1938. He often uses unconventional poetic forms to communicate dark or tragic messages.

Alden Nowlan (1933–1983) was a news editor, fiction writer and well-known poet who told stories of the people and places of his native Nova Scotia.

Frank O'Hara was an American poet who lived from 1926 to 1966. He created poem-paintings with New York artists.

Mary O'Neill (1908–1990) began her writing career as a copywriter for various advertising agencies. Writing primarily for young people, she published novels, short stories, and poetry, and contributed to magazines.

Richard Peck has written many novels for young adults, many drawn from his experiences as a high-school teacher. Peck was born in 1934 and lives in New York City.

Li Po was one of China's greatest poets and one of the most frequently translated into English. He lived from 701–762 during the T'ang dynasty.

Robert Priest is a Canadian writer, born in England in 1951. In addition to writing poetry, he has worked as a mail carrier, carpenter, shipper, and factory worker.

Rose Rauter contributed this poem to the *Riverside Anthology of Children's Literature* in 1985.

Kenneth Rexroth (1905–1982) worked as a labourer while writing poetry and painting. He uses many poetic techniques and themes.

Edwin Arlington Robinson (1869–1935) was a New England poet, known for his long narrative poems and shorter character sketches. He won the first Pulitzer Prize for poetry.

Tomas Santos was a seven-year-old boy from the Philippines when his poem "A Wish" was published in 1966.

F. R. Scott (1899–1985) wrote four volumes of poetry and translated two others. He also edited literary journals and poetry anthologies. He is from Québec.

Tsuboi Shigeji was born in 1889. A member of the Japan Proletarian Writers League, he was imprisoned twice for his political views.

Linda Shimizu was born in Vancouver in 1978. She started writing in grade seven as part of a young writers group in Burnaby.

Paul Simon was born in 1942 in New Jersey. Once part of the successful Simon and Garfunkel duo, he has produced many albums of his own.

Raymond Souster is a poet, anthology editor, and accountant born in 1921 in Toronto. He is known for his ability to find poetic elements in everyday life.

Myra Stilborn was born in Viceroy, Saskatchewan, and grew up in Indian Head. She contributes short stories and poetry to various Canadian publications.

May Swenson (1919–1989) was a Swedish-American poet whose first collection of poems was published in 1954. She often arranged poems on the page in ways that illustrated their meaning.

Jim Tallosi is a poet, born in 1947 in Hungary. When he was nine, his family moved to Winnipeg, Manitoba. He has written two books of poetry.

John Updike, born in 1932, launched his writing career by working for *The New Yorker* magazine writing reviews, poems, and stories. He is now best known for his novels and stories about suburban life.

Miriam Waddington's poems have been translated into many languages, and set to music. She was born in 1917 in Winnipeg, Manitoba.

Alice Walker (born in 1944) is an African-American novelist, short-story writer, and poet, best known for her Pulitzer Prize–winning novel *The Color Purple*.

William Carlos Williams (1883–1963) was a medical doctor throughout his life in New Jersey, while also writing poetry, plays, essays, and novels.

Valerie Worth was born in 1933 in Pennsylvania. She has been publishing books of poetry since 1971 and contributes poems to anthologies and magazines.

Hisaye Yamamoto was born in California in 1921. Her short stories have appeared in many magazines and journals.

Credits

Grateful acknowledgment is given to authors, publishers, and agents for permission to reprint the following copyrighted material. Every effort has been made to determine copyright owners. In the case of any omissions, the Publisher will be pleased to make suitable acknowledgments in future editions.

iii "Poetry" by Eleanor Farjeon appeared in *Wider than the Sky: Poems to Grow Up With* edited by Scott Elledge. Copyright © 1990 by Scott Elledge. Published by HarperCollins Publishers. Reprinted by permission of David Higham Associates, London.

1 From *The Darkening Fire* by Irving Layton. Reprinted by permission of the author.

2 Appeared in *Canadian Literature*, Number 124–125, Spring/Summer 1990.

3 From COLLECTED POEMS by Frank O'Hara. Copyright © 1967 by Maureen Granville-Smith, Administratrix of the Estate of Frank O'Hara. Reprinted by permission of Alfred A. Knopf, Inc.

4 From THE CARPENTERED HEN AND OTHER TAME CREATURES by John Updike. Copyright © 1957 by John Updike. Reprinted by permission of Alfred A. Knopf, Inc.

5 Copyright © 1969 by May Swenson. Used with permission of The Literary Estate of May Swenson.

6 From *Joyful Noise: Poems for Two Voices* by Paul Fleischman. Copyright © 1988 by Paul Fleischman. Selection reprinted by permission of HarperCollins Publishers.

8 "Warning: (A Found Poem)" appeared in *The Claremont Review*, copyright © 1992; "A Wish" is from *Miracles: Poems by Children of the English-Speaking World* edited by Richard Lewis, Copyright © 1991 by The Touchstone Center, New York.

9 From Richard Lewis, ed., *op. cit.*

10 From *Winning Monologs for Young Actors* by Peg Kehret. Copyright © 1986 Meriwether Publishing Ltd., Colorado Springs, CO. Used by permission.

14 Appeared in *The Next World: Poems by 32 Third World Americans* edited by Joseph Bruchac. Published by The Crossing Press.

15 From THE POEMS OF STANLEY KUNITZ by Stanley Kunitz. Copyright © 1971 by Stanley Kunitz. By permission of Little, Brown and Company.

17 From THE POEMS OF STANLEY KUNITZ 1928–1978 by Stanley Kunitz. Copyright © 1953 by Stanley Kunitz. First appeared in *New World Writing*. By permission of Little, Brown and Company.

18 From *Counterpoint* (Asian Studies Center, UCLA, 1976.) Copyright © 1976 by Hisaye Yamamoto DeSoto.

20 "The Future of Poetry in Canada" by Elizabeth Brewster is reprinted from *Selected Poems* by permission of Oberon Press.

22 "Great Things Have Happened" by Alden Nowlan, Irwin Publishing, is reprinted by permission of Stoddart Publishing Co. Limited, 34 Lesmill Road, Don Mills, Ontario.

24 Appeared in *Another Wordsandwich*, copyright © 1979 by Books by Kids. Reprinted by permission of Annick Press.

26 From *The Last Landscape*, copyright © Miriam Waddington 1992. Reprinted by permission of Oxford University Press Canada.

28 Copyright © 1976 by Moose Music Inc. Used by permission.

30 From *Children of the Night* by Edwin Arlington Robinson. (New York: Charles Scribner's Sons, 1897).

31 Copyright © 1966 Paul Simon. Used by permission of the publisher, Paul Simon Music.

32 From *The Poetry of Robert Frost* edited by Edward Connery Lathem. Copyright © 1916, 1923, 1928, 1930, 1934, 1939, 1969 by Henry Holt and Company Inc.

34 "I Go Along" by Richard Peck, copyright © 1989 by Richard Peck from CONNECTIONS: SHORT STORIES by Donald R. Gallo, Editor. Used by permission of Delacorte Press, a division of Bantam Doubleday Dell Publishing Group, Inc.

42 "Mississippi Winter IV" from HORSES MAKE A LANDSCAPE LOOK MORE BEAUTIFUL: POEMS BY ALICE WALKER, copyright © 1984 by Alice Walker, reprinted by permission of Harcourt Brace & Company.

43 From *The Penguin Book of Japanese Verse* translated by G. Bownas and A. Thwaite. Copyright © 1964 by Geoffrey Bownas and Anthony Thwaite. Published by Penguin Books, Inc. Reproduced by permission of Penguin Books Ltd.

44 Copyright © 1970, 1978, 1980, 1981 by Toni Cade Bambara. Reprinted by permission of the author.